# HOW IT ALL BEGA



"Dear Blue Peter,
I liked it when the lion yawned . . .
I liked the baboon sneaking up behind Princess Anne . . .
Why did Princess Anne ask you to go, anyway . . .?"

We had hundreds of letters like that after our film "Blue Peter Royal Safari", and everybody seemed to be asking the same question. Why was Blue Peter chosen to go on Safari with Princess Anne?

It all began last year with the Save the Children Fund. The Princess had just become their new President, and they asked if she would consent to appear in a film about the Fund's work in Kenya. The Princess evidently agreed, and after some discussions between the Save the Children Fund, Buckingham Palace and the BBC, the telephone rang in the Blue Peter office and a voice said: "Would you like to make a film with Princess Anne?"

By the end of the week, we were driving through the gates of Buckingham Palace to meet Bill Heseltine, the Queen's Press Secretary, and Mary Dawnay, one of Princess Anne's ladies-in-waiting. We were given coffee and talked for a while about the kind of film we hoped to make, while outside a band of the Household Division was playing selections from *Oklahoma* and the Guards were changing in the courtyard. Then the door opened, and Princess Anne herself came in.

It was difficult not to be impressed – apart from the fact that she's a Royal Princess, Princess Anne's also an extremely attractive girl with a radiant, friendly smile. After ten minutes' conversation, it was obvious that she also had a lively mind, a very definite point of view, and an enormous sense of humour.

Soon afterwards Air Commodore Archie Winskill, Captain of the Queen's Flight, arrived with the seating plan of the Royal Plane. The Queen's Flight

At 10.00 a.m. on Saturday, 6th February, 1971, a VC 10 of Air Support Command soared into the grey London sky outward bound for Nairobi. In the Royal suite, Princess Anne talked to Val about the different things she hoped to see and do on her first solo Royal visit.

consists of three Andovers, two Westland Wessex helicopters, and Prince Charles's Beagle Basset. They're all short-haul aircraft. When the Royal Family flies out on a long journey like the four thousand miles to Kenya, they sometimes "borrow" a VC 10 of Air Support Command, which has a special VIP fit. From the outside it seems just like an ordinary aeroplane, but part of the inside is divided into what looks like two cabins on a luxury liner. In the main one, instead of the usual aircraft seats, there's a horseshoe banquette with a low coffee table in front of it. At either side there are rackfuls of magazines and newspapers – the shaded table lamps would look more at home in a smart restaurant than a 500-mph jet!

On the wall are two clocks – one showing GMT, the other the local time of whichever part of the world the aircraft happens to be.

We were given permission to film while the aircraft was in flight and we had to show on the plan exactly where our cameras were going to be placed. It looked as though it was going to be an extremely tight squeeze. Even a Royal compartment looks pretty small when it's packed to the roof with film equipment.

Ten days later, we all met again – this time at the Alcock and Brown VIP lounge at London Airport. No one would have guessed it was a Royal flight until Air Commodore Archie Winskill arrived looking quite splendid in immaculately pressed khaki drill (despite the cold February morning) and covered from head to foot in gold tassels.

The Air Commodore stood at the foot of the steps, ready to take the salute as Princess Anne, followed by Val, boarded the aircraft. The Blue Peter camera crew took their place with the mass of press photographers, ready to take the first shot of the film. We were all feeling apprehensive – Val said later that the short walk across the tarmac with Princess Anne was one of the most terrifying moments of her life. The Princess seemed very calm and cheerful, but she must have been feeling a bit nervous, too – after all, this was not only her first solo Royal visit, but it was also her first solo Royal film. Later on, when Val asked if she ever had nerves, she admitted she had – but added: "I think the day you stop getting nerves means you're not doing your job as well as you should."

After take-off, the nervous tension was broken by the sheer farce of trying to present the camera crew to the Princess in a cabin full of film equipment. We had decided to set up the cameras for the first conversation before introducing Princess Anne to the crew. This proved to be a mistake, because once the cameras were in position, the Princess was trapped on one side of the cabin and there was scarcely room to move on the other. After the first man had climbed over a camera and a mass of cables, tried to bow and shake hands formally in the space the size of a postage stamp, and then crawled off on all fours under another camera to make room for the next man, we all dissolved into giggles, and that seemed to set the scene for the next ten days.

# WELCOME TO KENYA!

The visit to Gatundu, President Jomo Kenyatta's farm outside Nairobi, was an historic occasion. The Princess was joined by her brother, the Prince of Wales, who was on holiday in Kenya, for an official meeting with the President. It was rather moving to see that one-time enemy of Britain – now over 80 and still the most powerful and magnificent looking man in Africa welcoming two young members of the British Royal family, and obviously being completely charmed by them.

Gatundu was a hive of activity. Kikuyu tribesmen had been gathering since dawn, and when the Royal car arrived, the route to the President's house was lined by rows of chanting, clapping dancers.

On the compound in the heat of the midday African sun, a thousand tribesmen danced a tumultuous welcome to the Royal pair, and soon the Prince of Wales, Princess Anne and the President left the VIP stand and walked through clouds of dust right into the middle of the swirling dancers.

The President gave a speech of welcome in his own tribal language and the Prince of Wales replied in English. The President asked Princess Anne if she would speak to the crowds, and she delighted them by waving and saying "Jambo" – which means "hello". Afterwards, Princess Anne said it wasn't a very long speech, but it was the only word she knew in Swahili.

President Jomo Kenyatta laid on a tumultuous tribal welcome for the Royal party.

# BIG GAME

Only fifteen minutes' drive from the centre of Nairobi is the National Wildlife Park. But once you're through the gates, you could be thousands of miles from civilisation. As far as the eye can see, there are acres of gently undulating savannahs. Herds of wild zebra, antelope, giraffe and wildebeest are stalked by lions, cheetahs and leopards. We were told that the best time to see the wildlife was first thing in the morning – by midday all the animals are sleeping to escape the sun – so we met at the park gates as soon as it was light.

Princess Anne and Valerie are both keen photographers (in fact they both use the same make of camera) and Princess Anne has inherited an interest in wildlife from her father, the Duke of Edinburgh, who is the President of the World Wildlife Fund, and has been on Safari in Kenya himself quite recently.

We had what even the chief game warden, Mr Mohammed, who was our guide and driver, described as a "lucky day". It was lucky for us on two counts, firstly because Blue Peter cameraman Ken Westbury got some really memorable shots of the big game, and secondly because Princess Anne and Val were so engrossed by the wildlife, they completely forgot about the camera that was photographing *them*.

We were driving along a deserted track when all at once we saw something move in the grass only a few feet away from the Land Rover – it was not one lion, but a whole pride, basking in the sun. "Look at his big, yellow eyes," whispered Princess Anne as a huge,

In Nairobi National Park, Princess Anne and Valerie were given special permission to photograph the game from an open-topped Land Rover.

Ken Westbury, our Blue Peter cameraman, wasn't the only one to get good pictures. Princess Anne didn't do too badly. Ken was quite impressed! "Princess Anne has a good eye for a picture and a real sense of composition. She's also very quick at grabbing interesting action pictures – like her smashing shot of a yawning lioness."

Princess Anne and Val were so engrossed by the wild life, they completely forgot about the camera that was photographing *them*. "Hey you – King of the Jungle – what are you walking away for?" said Princess Anne as a lion slunk off into the bush.

maned head appeared over a tuft of grass. A sleepy lioness stretched her front paws, gave an enormous yawn, and Princess Anne clicked her shutter at exactly the right moment to get – as she remarked – "a classic photo of lion yawning." The lion suddenly got bored by the whole thing and ambled off into the bush. "Hey you – King of the jungle – what are you walking away for?" said the Princess.

Later on we saw a herd of giraffe by a salt lick, and Princess Anne said: "I read in my book that they're ideally suited for necking – which they do all the time and with either sex – they're not worried about it!"

But perhaps our luckiest sight was a mother cheetah with four tiny cubs stumbling after her. It would have been worth the trip for that alone, because we were told cheetahs don't breed in captivity, so it's only in the wild that there's a chance to see a mother with its young. They looked very safe and cuddly, but Mr Mohammed kept the engine of the Land Rover running – just in case. Cheetahs are the fastest animals on four legs, and the mother could run down her prey at anything up to 75 mph.

By the time the sun had risen, we'd seen over ten different species of big game. But there was more to come. At the gates of the Game Reserve there's a special orphanage for baby animals who've lost their parents. Generally, as soon as they can safely fend for themselves, they're released into the reserve. But occasionally, one or two steadfastly refuse to go – and stay on as big game pets. Julian Tong, the curator, showed Princess Anne and Val a baby leopard and an amazingly tame half-grown cheetah. In the wild, the leopard takes precedence over the cheetah who will always wait respectfully for the bigger cat to finish feeding before moving in on the kill. The young cheetah at the orphanage was a good deal older and bigger than the baby leopard who was a tiny, cuddly creature, but as soon as Princess Anne stroked the cheetah, the leopard cub went absolutely beserk – hissing and snarling and spitting. He evidently decided that princesses should observe jungle law and stroke leopards before they stroke cheetahs!

1 & 2. In the Animal Orphanage at the entrance to the park, Princess Anne made friends with a baby leopard and fed the resident rhinoceros.

3 Mr Mohammad, the chief game warden, knew where all the most interesting animals were likely to be found.

1

3

2

# RIDING

Everyone knows that Princess Anne is a very keen horsewoman, although few people realise how serious she is about her one real hobby, yet she manages to devote a tremendous amount of time and energy to riding – without being in the slightest degree a horsey type. For this reason, we wanted to include a riding sequence in our film, with Princess Anne telling Val all about her ambitions as a three-day event rider who may one day end up representing her country in the Olympic Games.

Our riding location couldn't have been a more perfect setting – we chose a grassy track bordering acres of coffee plantations, which led through a eucalyptus grove to an enormous double field where it would be possible to ride at full gallop. Colonel Brian Tayleur lent us two of his polo ponies for the day – Princess Anne rode a spirited grey called Silver Tip, Valerie's chestnut was Waif and looked quieter, but we were all in for a surprise – as we were to find out before long!

Princess Anne and Valerie gave the horses a canter before reining them in, and as they walked between the rows of shiny green coffee bushes, Valerie asked – "How many horses have you got?"

*Princess Anne*
I've got three really. One is actually mine which was given to me, which is my first one.

*Valerie*
Is he your favourite?

*Princess Anne*
Well, he's actually a great character you know – he's got a lot to say for himself. The other two really belong to my mother – both home bred, but they're so different, you can't help liking them.

*Valerie*
You take part a lot in competitions and show jumping and things like that?

*Princess Anne*
Not, strictly speaking, show jumping. I call myself an eventer, which means I do these three-day event larks which involves a phase of dressage and cross-country and show jumping.

*Valerie*
So it involves more really than just being a show jumper?

*Princess Anne*
Well, you do everything – it's not specialised and I think you enjoy it almost more that way.

Discussing the next shot with the crew on location at Loresho Ridge.

Princess Anne rode a spirited grey polo pony called Silver Tip. Val's chestnut was Waif, and looked quieter – but we were all in for a surprise!

*Valerie*
Do you get a chance to take part in a lot of big events? I think you were in the Horse of the Year Show, weren't you – about two years ago?
*Princess Anne*
Not with any conspicuous success – it was dressage and show jumping. Jumping inside for a horse is very strange if you've only ever done it outside, you know.
*Valerie*
If you weren't a Princess, do you think you'd like to have taken up, perhaps not show jumping, but any form of competition work professionally?
*Princess Anne*
I think on the whole I might have found myself a sort of reasonable job if I hadn't been a Princess – but I think I would always want to do it in some small way.
*Valerie*
Do you have any ambitions left that you want to do as far as riding is concerned?
*Princess Anne*
It would be very nice to take part in the Olympics, but then that's quite a big goal you know. But I think one must have an ambition if one's going to be a sportsman of any kind, and I think that's what one would work for – then I have a very able trainer, and I think she has her sights on that, too!
*Valerie*
Didn't you ride those fantastic horses in Austria at the Spanish Riding School? I think you're the only woman to have done that, aren't you?
*Princess Anne*
My mother had ridden them once before, but in London. I think I was the first person to ride them actually in Vienna.
*Valerie*
Was it very difficult?
*Princess Anne*
I think with a basic knowledge of dressage you can

Two high spots – riding a Lippizaner at the famous Spanish Riding School in Vienna, and competing in the 1970 Knowlton Horse Trials.

just about do it – but very exciting – it's a very unusual thing to do.

*Valerie*

That's a challenge, isn't it, as well?

*Princess Anne*

Oh, very much so – dressage isn't exactly my strong point!

*Valerie*

It certainly isn't mine – my strong point's just about being able to stay on, I think.

Val was being modest. Contrary to reports that appeared in the Press, she's quite an experienced rider. Not in the Princess Anne class of course – but she has been riding since her childhood and still rides in Richmond Park as often as she has the time to spare. Her famous "fall" was certainly not due to bad horsemanship, but very bad luck. Shortly after this conversation, Val was following Princess Anne at full gallop across a field. Suddenly there was the roar of an engine, and a large red tractor appeared driving directly across their path. This coincided with Princess Anne and Val having to make a sharp turn round a clump of eucalyptus trees, and Val's horse had such a fright, he threw her and galloped off as fast as he could – following Princess Anne who was slightly in front. Val took an extremely nasty fall, and although she was lucky not to have been seriously injured, she bit her tongue very badly. It says a lot for her professionalism that she was back in the saddle only half an hour after the accident.

BBC rules stipulate that any accident to an artist on location must be properly reported on the correct form. The form was duly completed and section 14 reads:

Name of witnesses (and addresses if not members of staff:)

H.R.H. The Princess Anne
Buckingham Palace, The Mall, S.W.1.

# KIKUYU VILLAGE

Although there are big, modern cities in Kenya – the small villages have scarcely changed for thousands of years. Clusters of huts with thatched beehive roofs cling to hillsides or squat in valleys – so perfectly camouflaged they blend unobtrusively with the surrounding trees and bushes. Princess Anne and Val had just crossed a stream in what appeared to be an isolated part of the country when they stumbled on a village nestling on the other side of the bridge.

A crowd of children ran out from the huts – they were smiling and giggling and overwhelmed with curiosity – not because a Royal Princess had come to see them (they had no idea who the visitors were) but because Kenyans are some of the friendliest people in the world, and delight in meeting strangers.

There was a mixture of girls and boys of all shapes and sizes from tiny toddlers who could only walk a few steps before sitting down on the ground, to 11- and 12-year-olds, some of whom spoke a little English. There were cheerful exchanges of "Jambo" and then

Kenyans are some of the friendliest people in the world. These children ran out to greet Princess Anne and Val, proudly showing them their new puppy.

one of the older boys held up a very small puppy and described the two-month-old litter that had been born to one dog in the village.

It looked an idyllic scene – a carefree outdoor life, happy children playing in the sun – but the Princess told Val that there is little for the children to do. When they are old enough, they must work in the fields and most of them have no hope of any kind of education. In hundreds of similar villages all over Kenya, the children have one burning ambition – to run away to Nairobi, where – like modern Dick Whittingtons – they believe they will be able to find fame and fortune and help not only themselves, but their poverty-stricken families.

To the children, the visitors were just two strangers on horseback. They had no idea they were talking to a Royal Princess!

# STAREHE TO THE RESCUE

In 1958, 25-year-old Geoffrey Griffin was so appalled by the sight of ragged seven- and eight-year-olds destitute in the streets of Nairobi, he took six of the waifs into the shelter of two tin huts – and the Starehe Boys' Centre was founded.

Now there are over a thousand pupils at the school, housed in a vast complex of modern buildings including a large Assembly Hall where the boys meet every day, laboratories, a spacious dining-room, a technical division including workshops and an impressive library called the Decagon.

This unusual school is one of the greatest success stories in Africa, and it is supported by a number of philanthropic individuals and organisations – including the Save the Children Fund. Princess Anne asked Val if she would join her on an official visit, in her capacity as President of the Fund, and the British High Commissioner in Kenya, Sir Eric Norris, introduced Geoffrey Griffin, Starehe's director – the man whose insight, drive and compassion made the whole school possible.

We were lucky enough to be able to film the complete story of how children make their first contact with the school – and it all starts, not in the smart modern classrooms at Starehe, but in a ramshackle building in a poor district of Nairobi – the Save the Children Fund Rescue Centre.

One evening, Princess Anne and Val joined a queue of destitute children waiting outside the Rescue Centre. At 7.30 sharp, the doors were opened and the queue poured inside, across a cobbled yard and over to rows of rough benches and wooden tables. All the boys were waifs who had somehow or other made their way to Nairobi to seek their fortunes. But their chances were hopeless from the start. The ones not picked up by the police become beggars and resort to lives of petty crime to keep alive. They become disease-ridden – riddled with ringworm and suffering badly from malnutrition. But news spreads by word of mouth that at the Rescue Centre you can get a free meal and a night's sleep and no one's ever turned away. The whole place is kept deliberately scruffy so as not to scare away the timid, and the children can continue to have free food and lodging for up to three weeks, before having to make up their

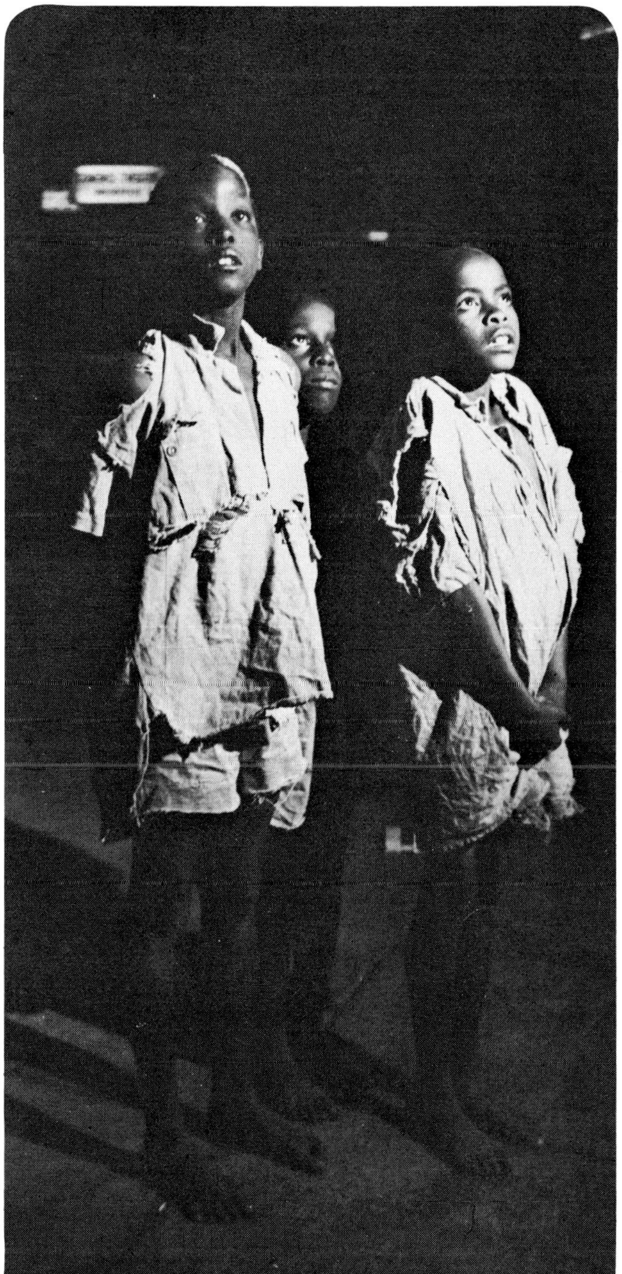

Children leave their villages to seek fame and fortune – lured by the bright lights of Nairobi. But life is hard and bewildering in this big city.

The lucky ones find food and shelter at the Save the Children Fund Rescue Centre. Princess Anne and Val talked to some of the boys and their interpreter was 15-year-old Joseph who had himself come to the Centre when he was eight, and alone and destitute in Nairobi.

minds whether or not to agree to go to the Starehe School's Place of Safety – the next stage in the chain of rehabilitation.

Joseph – a boy of fifteen and hoping to become a doctor, who had himself been a destitute waif seven years earlier, acted as interpreter for Princess Anne and Val. The boys came from all over Kenya and spoke a variety of tribal languages. Whilst generous helpings of soup, and a sort of dough made from flour and water were being ladled into metal bowls, Princess Anne said:

"Joseph, you couldn't ask them how far they've come to Nairobi – could you?"

Joseph turned to one of the boys called Kariuki and discovered he'd travelled over a hundred miles.

*Joseph*
How did you come here?

*Kariuki*
I came by bus.

*Joseph*
And where did you get the money?

*Kariuki*
I told the conductor I was going to see a lady in Nairobi – that she would be waiting at the bus stop with the money. But there was no lady, and I ran away before the conductor could punish me.

*Joseph*
What do you want to do after the meal?

*Kariuki*
I just want to go to sleep.

*Joseph*
When you are at Starehe, what do you want to do?

*Kariuki*
I want to learn so hard.

*Princess Anne*
But Joseph, when you first came here, did you just spend one night here?

*Joseph*
I can remember – I spent about four nights, and then I went to the Place of Safety.

Princess Anne told Val the Rescue Centre was kept deliberately scruffy so as not to scare away the timid.

# THE PLACE OF SAFETY

This part of Geoff Griffin's carefully planned scheme is breathing space. Here the waifs are given the care and attention they so desperately need – but before being made full members of the school, case workers track down every scrap of information they can find so that they can decide what to do in the best interests of each child. They travel many miles, visiting the villages the children have run away from to find out if the parents are alive – sometimes they discover the parents are dead, or that the mother is newly widowed and her eldest son has set out intent on somehow finding money to support her and his brothers and sisters. Sometimes the father may be alive, but ill or injured and unable to work.

Many children run away specifically to try and scrape an education that will enable them to earn their living and help to support their families. Education in Kenya is not free – and a bereaved family can hardly ever continue to pay school fees.

Unbelievable as it seems – children even younger than the six-year-old we filmed having his medical examination are sometimes brought to the Place of Safety. The little boy we filmed was called Kimani and he stared at us unflinching with his big brown eyes as the doctor made him put out his tongue and the nurse weighed and measured him. But even the newest, smallest boy will feel loved and cared for at Starehe. Geoff Griffin told us of a five-year-old who

The boys are taken from the Rescue Centre to the Place of Safety while their cases are being investigated.

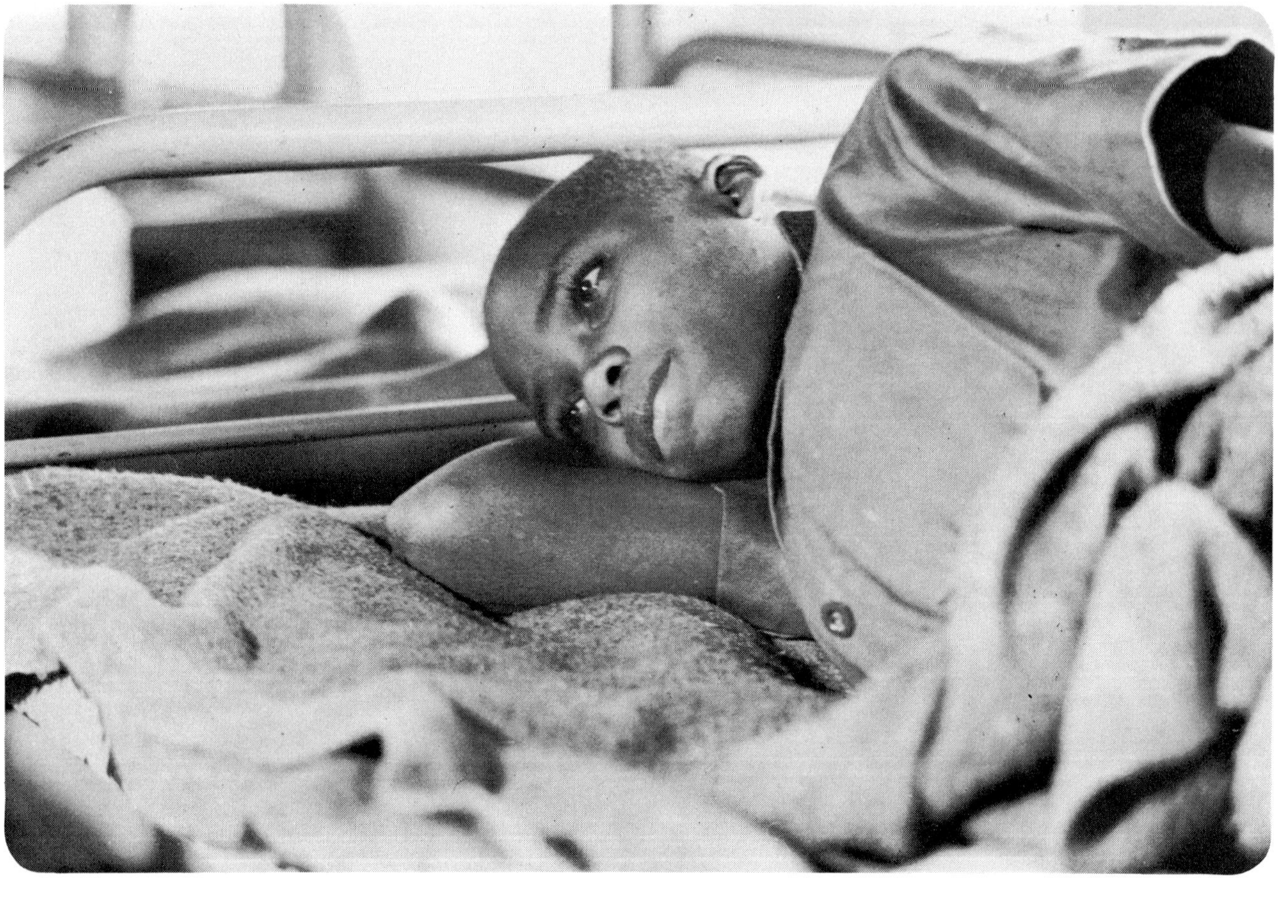

had been found wandering in the Nairobi streets by the police. No one could understand the few words he spoke – it wasn't even possible to tell from which tribe he came. But although it was Sunday, a time when the boys are free to do what they please, there was never a moment when the child was left alone. Two or three boys were constantly at his side, and as soon as one left, another took his place. They could not talk to the child, but by their presence and friendliness, they managed to make him feel safe and welcome and among friends. All of this was entirely spontaneous – with no direction from any of the masters.

Research by the case workers may take as long as six months, and during that time the "Brown coat" boys have lessons just like the other members of the school. To break down the barriers of the different tribal languages, English is one of the first things the new boys are taught. And quite often, the Primary classes are held out of doors.

"Aren't they lucky! It only happened to me once in my life," said Princess Anne as she and Val watched a class in progress under the warm African sun.

There was no question of the boys being distracted by the visitors. They didn't take their eyes off their master for a second, and each time he asked a question – holding out different objects for the boys to identify – a sea of hands swished through the air.

"They lap up every crumb of information," one of the masters told us, and there was no doubt that contrary to many schools in Britain, lessons at Starehe are regarded as a passport that will take a child from poverty, to a life of comfort and luxury beyond the wildest dreams of his parents in their thatched beehive hut.

"They stay at the Place of Safety until they've been resettled – or, if they have absolutely no relations, and no hope of going home, they will eventually swop these brown uniforms for the smart red shirts and blue shorts of the Starehe School, of which they're very proud," Princess Anne told Valerie. And in a very short space of time, the children become remarkably fluent speakers and writers of what, after all, is a foreign language for most of them.

After a donation of tinned puddings from a food factory, Sammy Owino, who was only eight years old, wrote in the school magazine:

"One day before I went to play football, I filled my stomach with a whole tin of Magic Pudding and I didn't feel tired the whole afternoon. So I think we should always give these puddings to our teams if we want to defeat other schools. These puddings make small boys grow big, and lean boys grow fat!"

Football is one of the most popular games played at the School. And when Princess Anne and Val joined a crowd of boys watching an inter-school match, they were amazed to see the players all had bare feet!

The Starehe boys play hockey, basketball and tennis, as well as football, and they also have thriving archery and rifle clubs. But one game that completely baffled both Princess Anne and Val was "African Draughts". It was played by two boys using a long, wooden board with hollowed-out circles in two parallel rows. The boys scraped pebbles in and out of the hollows with incredible speed – and the winner was the boy who ended up with most pebbles. We only showed about twenty seconds of African Draughts on BLUE PETER ROYAL SAFARI, but afterwards letters came flooding in from all over Britain. People said the game was called "Warri" or "Mancala", or "Bao" or "Sungka" or "Maugala", and Mr Fowlds of West Wickham even said he'd invented his own version!

As the game is thousands of years old, it was interesting to see how it had spread to different corners of the world – with different names and different rules. And now you can even get it as a board game in Britain.

Princess Anne told Val of the enormous prestige of being a "Starehe" boy. Geoff Griffin had the good idea of accepting 10% fee-paying pupils – so that there would never be any stigma attached to having had a Starehe education. But far from being stigmatised, the boys – with their opportunities for learning English, French, German, Physics, Maths – to say nothing of Mechanical Engineering and Agricultural Science – are the envy of all other children. Competition for the few fee-paying places

To break down the barriers of the different tribal languages, English is one of the first things the new boys are taught.

Every new boy is given a bath and a thorough medical examination.

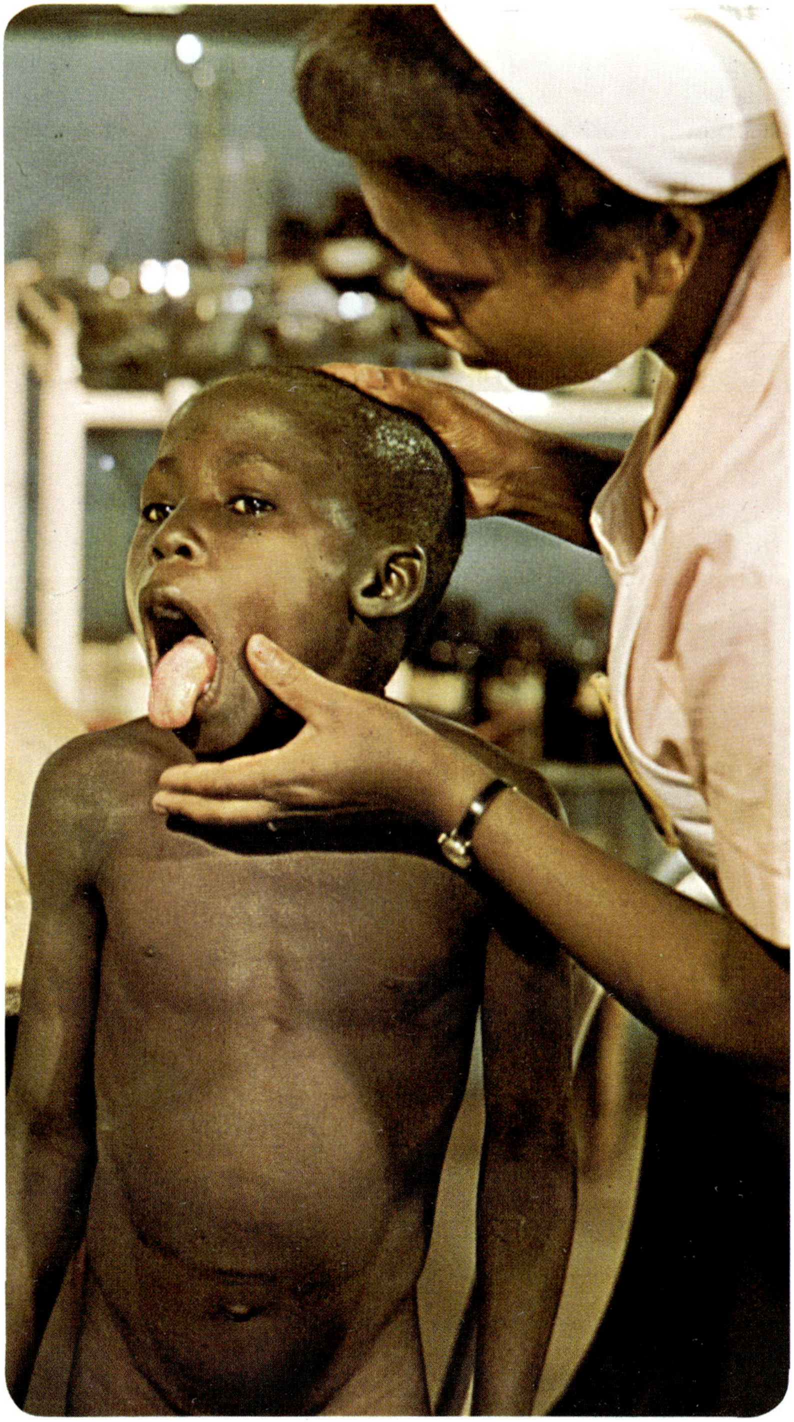

is fierce, and the lucky pupils include the grandson of President Jomo Kenyatta.

A smart invitation card arrived whilst we were in Nairobi:

"On the occasion of the Visit of H.R.H. The Princess Anne, the Director, Staff and Pupils of the Starehe Boys' Centre request the pleasure of the company of the Blue Peter Team to a dinner at the School at 7.30 p.m. and afterwards to an Entertainment."

By special request, Princess Anne wore a dazzling, full-length, gold and white evening gown on the night of the Starehe Entertainment. Some of the younger boys hadn't believed she was a real, live Princess when they'd seen her in her cotton mini skirt! After a splendid, four-course dinner in the new Dining Hall including "Roast leg of Molo Lamb" and "Tropical Fruit Salad", we took our seats out of

These workshops are the pride of Starehe. Here the boys are fitting a new engine into a Land Rover.

Because some of the younger boys hadn't believed she was a real, live Princess, Princess Anne wore a dazzling, gold and white evening dress on the night of the Starehe Entertainment.

More than six different tribes are represented at the school, and each one performed their own tribal dance to entertain the Royal visitor.

doors – the floodlights were switched on, the band played and a troupe of boys snaked their way across the grass in the traditional tribal costume. Joseph led the Kamba tribe in an imposing outfit of feathers and war-paint. It was hard to recognise him as our interpreter from the Place of Safety! There were eight different tribal dances, lots of rousing songs, and special pieces from the band. Altogether, it was a memorable evening. Geoff Griffin found the whole thing almost unbelievable.

"I never imagined," he said, standing by the two famous tin huts that housed the first pupils of the school, "in 1958, that twelve years later a Princess would be our guest of honour!"

# TREETOPS

Treetops, a unique tree house, built especially for wild game spotting, has been famous ever since 1952 when a young girl climbed up its wooden ladder a Princess, and the following day climbed down a Queen – our own Queen Elizabeth II. It was a moving moment during our filming when Princess Anne retold the story of her grandfather's death and how – contrary to popular belief – her mother didn't hear the news of her accession until she had actually left Treetops, and had returned to Sagana Lodge, some twenty miles away. Princess Anne pointed out to Val the site of the original Treetops where the Queen stayed. This was burnt down a few years ago, and the present Treetops is considerably bigger.

This historical flashback was brought abruptly to a halt by a series of earsplitting shrieks. Richard and Gladys had arrived for tea! We'd been warned beforehand what was likely to happen at baboon feeding time – "mischievous thieves" was how Colonel Hayes-Newington, the resident White Hunter, described them. "Guard your handbags, sunglasses and camera – and keep your windows tightly shut until dark." And it was exceedingly difficult to believe Princess Anne's story of a friend whose young child, grabbed by an elderly baboon, was miraculously saved from being hurled over the edge of the thirty-five-foot-high observation platform.

After five minutes of baboon dodging, we'd have believed anything. Princess Anne's maid, who arrived late and missed the Colonel's warning about locking windows, was startled to see a dark, hairy figure emptying a suitcase on to her bed!

The big game like Elephants and Rhinos don't usually come to drink at the water hole and dig for salt until nightfall. There are floodlights on the side of the verandah which gradually fade up as darkness falls, so that the animals aren't scared away. But during the afternoon, Buffalo wander across the forest to drink – they look like large cows, although they can be unexpectedly dangerous when roused! During the day, in fact, it's quite easy to forget one's in Africa and be lulled into a state of false security. For instance, when we arrived, we had to park our Land Rover 200 yards away and walk through what looked like a peaceful English spinney. To our surprise, we were taken under armed escort! And all along the path there were "blinds" – tough wooden screens – to dodge behind should a marauding rhino

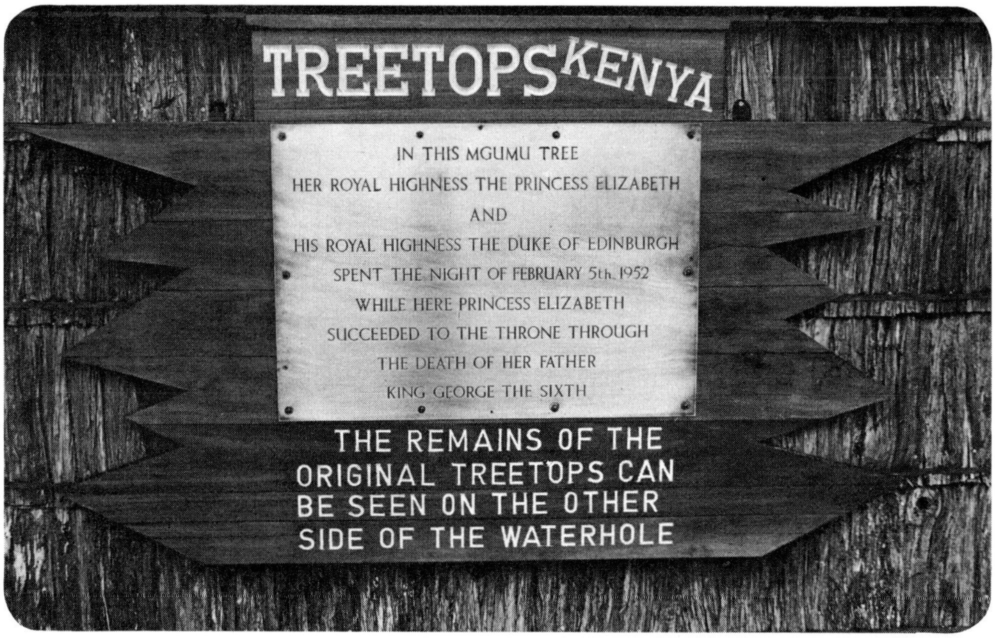

become too inquisitive! The last blind is only about five yards away from the wooden stairs of Treetops and is the scene of one of the White Hunter's most famous stories. Three years before Princess Anne's visit, the hunter was bringing up a visitor when they were charged by a cow elephant. The elephant was in a frenzy about her calf who was stuck in the mud of the water hole – the hunter and his visitor managed to run for the blind, but the whole of the wall was broken by the enraged elephant – and at the last second, the hunter had to shoot her dead at a range of four feet. The visitor, an elderly Australian lady, was in a state of considerable shock, but at least she was alive, and after hearing this tale, we are less inclined to scoff at the presence of the armed guard!

Princess Anne and Val settled themselves on the verandah to watch the game from a safe distance – and while they were waiting for dusk to fall, Valerie asked:

"I don't suppose you were very old, were you, when your mother became the Queen?"

*Princess Anne*
No – I suppose I wasn't – only about eighteen months. I don't remember very much at all.

*Valerie*
And the Coronation was – what, about fourteen months later, wasn't it?

Treetops is a unique hotel built in the branches of a Mgumu tree. Visitors come from all over the world to spot the wild game, and we were taken under armed escort through the bush to spend the night there.

The big game like Elephants and Rhino don't usually come to drink at the water hole until nightfall. But during the afternoon, Buffalo wander across the forest. They look like large cows, but can be unexpectedly dangerous when roused!

Princess Anne and Val were joined for tea by the baboons. "They'll pinch anything, so guard your handbags, sunglasses and cameras – and keep your windows locked until nightfall," warned the White Hunter.

*Princess Anne*
Yes, it was during the following year.
*Valerie*
Do you remember anything about it?
*Princess Anne*
Not very much – except for the normal sisterly fury at being left behind when my brother went to the Coronation.
*Valerie*
So you weren't allowed to go at all?
*Princess Anne*
I wasn't allowed to go and yet he went – which was the source of, and has been for the rest of my life, severe argument.
*Valerie*
It would have been marvellous. I actually spent the night in Hyde Park with a lot of school friends around a tree and it began to rain in the middle of the night. I remember, after the Queen had gone past, I went down to Buckingham Palace and saw you all come out on the balcony.
*Princess Anne*
Even me. Yes, I was allowed out for that but practically nothing else, and I distinctly remember having to play with a lot of invited, ahem, friends of roughly the same age which was anathema to me at that stage. I couldn't bear them!
*Valerie*
What's the first big occasion you remember?
*Princess Anne*
No idea! I really have absolutely none at all. I don't think I could put my finger on anything in particular that I've ever consciously started remembering anything by.
*Valerie*
Was it being a bridesmaid, or something like that?
*Princess Anne*
I don't remember so, funnily enough. I was a bridesmaid often enough, thank you very much – five times in all in under four years, which I thought was a bit excessive.
*Valerie*
I still find, although I've been doing "Blue Peter" for quite a long time, that every now and again I get some butterflies in my tummy. Do you find there are certain things that make you feel a little bit nervous – like perhaps making a speech or appearing at some big occasion?
*Princess Anne*
I think that practically anything you do if you stop having nerves – then really you know, you're not doing the job as well as you ought to. I think if you have a fit of nerves, you do that job that bit better.
*Valerie*
I agree.
*Princess Anne*
I think you always have nerves – you must do!
*Valerie*
You've got three brothers. What's it like being one sister amongst a large family?
*Princess Anne*
I was delighted I didn't have a sister, that's all!
*Valerie*
Really? Do you find it's made you more of a tomboy – when you were being brought up?
*Princess Anne*
Well – not the other two because I was only ten when

the next one turned up, and nearly fourteen – thirteen and a half, when the last one turned up.

*Valerie*

There's quite a big gap. Do you find that you get along with them very well? Do you find yourself being big sister and trying to keep them in order?

*Princess Anne*

I think you can't help being big sister with that sort of gap in age, because you know (*smiling*) you always consider that they're not getting the sort of discipline that you got when you were small so that is bad enough to start with.

*Valerie*

Obviously, both you and Prince Charles are very busy going all over the world doing different things. Do you get much of a chance to see each other?

*Princess Anne*

Well, I suppose we don't really. I mean, we live in the same house, at opposite ends of the corridor, but that's roughly speaking all. He usually goes out at different times of the day. But – normally speaking, the normal sort of school holidays which we stick to because of the two younger brothers, we see quite a lot of each other – and then, roughly speaking, that's enough, quite frankly. (*laughing*)

*Valerie*

You always make a tremendous impression with your fabulous outfits and hats – do you take a tremendous interest in clothes?

*Princess Anne*

Well, I'm delighted you think so – it's always a total mystery to me when I'm described as a sort of fashion leader, or anything else for that matter! I mean, clothes are part of the job, you have to have them . . . if you see what I mean – if you could describe it as a job. But you can't get many sort of fun clothes. I mean, people complain that you're not "with it" enough, but honestly – there's a limit to what you can do.

*Valerie*

What do you think of shorts?

*Princess Anne*

That's the limit! The absolute limit!

*Valerie*

I think I agree with you. I know I won't be wearing them.

*Princess Anne*

There are certain things I will not do – not even . . .

*Valerie*

All right for the beach – but not mid-winter.

Little did Val think – when she mentioned "shorts" that the nation's press would substitute "hot pants" and that Princess Anne's comments would be quoted in nearly every national newspaper!

On the surface the sea looked flat and ordinary, but under the water was a strange, silent and beautiful world.

# GOGGLING AT SHIMONE

In Nairobi, every day had been like an English summer's day. It's high and there's no humidity. But down on the coast, it's hot and lush and tropical, and the beaches are beautiful beyond belief. We filmed a goggling sequence with Princess Anne (doing it for the first time), and Valerie wearing snorkels and looking down into the water at the coral gardens.

On the surface the sea looked flat and ordinary, but under the water was a strange, silent, beautiful world. The coral clusters are in purple and violet, and amber, and weaving through them are millions of tropical fish in every colour under the sun.

There are occasional sharks in the Indian Ocean, so just to make sure all was safe we asked a frogman to patrol beneath the surface with a harpoon gun at the ready. We didn't mention this to anyone so as not to cause unnecessary alarm, but Princess Anne hadn't been in the water five minutes before she bobbed up and said:

"There's a strange man down there with a harpoon

There was time for sunbathing as well as goggling.

gun – did you know?"

At that moment, the diver broke the surface, and someone with great presence of mind said: "Ma'am, may I present Mr Peter Phillips – the diver." He must have been the first man who arrived from the bottom of the sea to be presented to a Royal Princess.

Filming swimming from a boat is fraught with difficulty at the best of times, but on that particular day everything seemed to be against us. The wind was swinging the camera boat everywhere but the right direction. Unexpected waves appeared from nowhere, soaking the cameras and microphones. We were all going frantic when Princess Anne pushed her mask back from her face and said:

"It's no good shouting at the sea – Canute couldn't stop it, what makes you think you can?"

To reach the coral reef, we went five miles out to sea by catamaran.

The sun was so fierce, Princess Anne and Val had to wear cotton shirts over their swim-suits.

# GOODBYE STAREHE

In eight days, we'd covered thousands of miles and met hundreds of people. Now, our Safari was nearly over, but there was one important thing to do before we left Kenya. The boys of Starehe have a weekly dance and Princess Anne and Val had promised to join them in the crowded Assembly Hall. And it was at the dance that the whole atmosphere of Blue Peter Royal Safari was summed up – not by Geoff Griffin or one of the masters, but by an eleven-year-old Starehe boy.

"The Princess," he said, watching H.R.H. dancing to an old Chubby Checker record, surrounded by a smiling crowd of boys – "the Princess, she is so sociable!"